7 painting pots

8 apples

9 boats

10 socks

The **First Skills** series includes seven books designed to help parents amuse, interest and at the same time teach their children. **Colours and shapes** and **abc** contribute to the child's early understanding of the reading process. **Counting** teaches her to recognize and understand simple numbers. **Telling the time** helps her to relate the time on a clock face to her everyday life and activities. **Big and little** deals with words that describe relative sizes and positions, all shown through objects and scenes that will be familiar to the young child. **Everyday words** helps her to enjoy and practise her vocabulary. **Verbs** will develop her early reading and language skills. In each book, bright, detailed, interesting illustrations combine with a simple and straightforward text to present fundamental concepts clearly and comprehensibly.

Help your child to say the number and trace over the number shape with a finger. Encourage her to touch what she is counting and, if possible, move the objects around and touch and count them again. Try making numbers from play dough. Finally, bring counting into your conversations: 'let's go down the stairs now, one, two, three!' 'How many bricks do we need to build this house? Let's count them!'

A catalogue record for this book is available form the British Library

Published by Ladybird Books Ltd
80 Strand London WC2R 0RL
A Penguin Company

2 4 6 8 10 9 7 5 3 1
© LADYBIRD BOOKS LTD MMVI

LADYBIRD and the device of a Ladybird are trademarks of Ladybird Books Ltd

Printed in Italy

counting

by Lesley Clark
photography by Garie Hind

1 one

one teddy bear

2 two

3 three

three cars

4 four

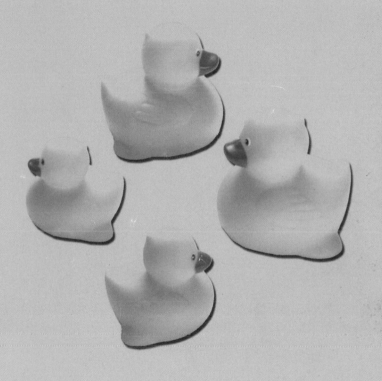

four ducks

5 *five*

five toothbrushes

6 six

six building blocks

7 seven

seven painting pots

8 eight

eight apples

9 nine

nine boats

Encourage your child to point to each boat as she counts it.

10 ten

ten socks

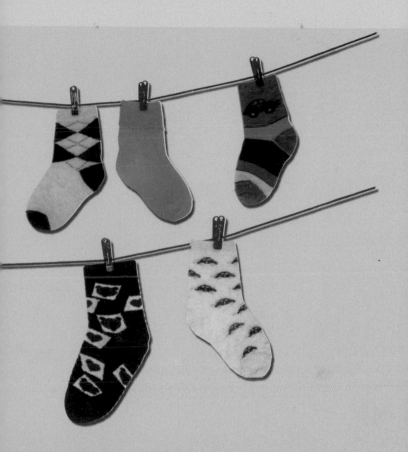

Count the socks and try to match the pairs on the line. You could do this at home with real socks or other objects.

What can you see in this bag?
How many are there of each thing?

Can you help to unpack the shopping?

Is everything here?

Here is the washing to sort out.

Let's get everything out of the basket.

How many T-shirts can you count?

How many socks?

Each of these boxes has three ducks. Can you count them?

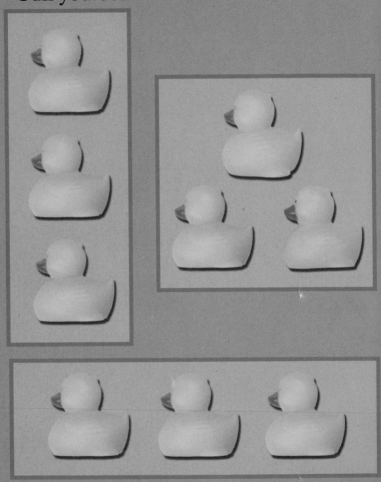

Play games with buttons and other objects to help your child understand that the number stays the same no matter how the objects are arranged.

How many drinks are there?

Is there a straw for each drink?

How many horses are on the farm?

How many cows?

How many geese?

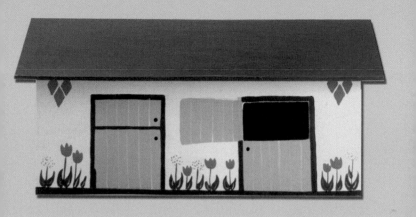

Count up all the animals and say
how many there are altogether.

These four cars drive round
and round.

These four are home –
safe and sound.

What games do you play with
your cars?

How many balls?

Which is the largest?

Which is the smallest?

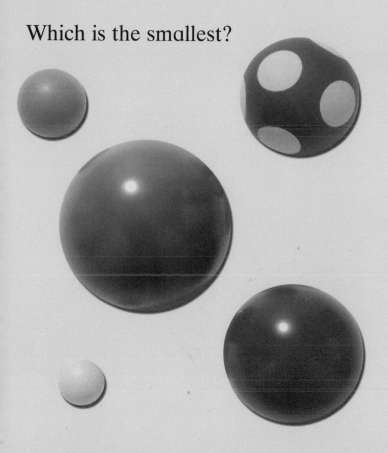

Talk about the different sizes and colours of the balls.

Can you count how many flowers?

Which one is different from all
the others?

Yum! How many green diamonds
are on the cake?

How many red diamonds?

How many are there altogether?

First Skills

Ideal for children aged 2 years and upwards, the **First Skills** readers, activity books and flash cards are designed for parents to help young children develop basic skills in early maths, language and writing.

Readers

Flash cards